A PONY CLUB PUBLICATION

Correct Dress for Riding

THE BRITISH HORSE SOCIETY
and THE PONY CLUB

© 1986 The Pony Club

Photographs by Kit Houghton
Design by Victor K. Shreeve

Published by The Pony Club

Designed, produced and distributed by
Threshold Books Limited, 661 Fulham Road, London SW6 5PZ

ISBN 0 900226 30 7

Typeset by York House Typographics Ltd

Printed in Great Britain by Martin's of Berwick

The Pony Club and Threshold Books acknowledge with
thanks the help given in the production of this
book by Mrs Laurence Rook, Mrs Tim Holderness-Roddam
and Mr Richard Meade.

CONTENTS

Introduction

A good rider takes pride in his own appearance as well as that of his horse. A neat, clean and correct turnout is not only a pleasing sight but it also makes practical sense because it encourages safe and effective riding.

To enjoy riding and to give the maximum assistance to your horse you must be comfortable. Your clothes need not be new – or even of top quality, though this will last longer – but it is essential that they fit well, and that, where appropriate (e.g. in the case of hats and footwear) they comply with safety standards.

In the Pony Club every effort is made to ensure that members wear correct dress for the various activities in which they take part.

The aim of this book is to provide acceptable guide-lines, both for beginners and for those riding at a higher level.

GENERAL NOTES

HATS

Crash Hats

Under Pony Club rules, members must wear hard hats at all times when mounted – at Pony Club rallies, in competitions, and during other activities. As from 1 January 1986 it is compulsory under Pony Club rules to wear a hat of BSI 4472 specification in all Pony Club **competitions**. This may be a jockey skull (generally worn with a 'silk' or other cover) or one of the other hats made to BSI 4472 specification.

- It is the Pony Club's view that the jockey skull (more popularly known as a 'crash hat') provides the best available protection, and because of the interior padding in the headband is the easiest to fit and the most comfortable to wear. The Pony Club intends that this should become the normal headgear for all activities, but that for the time being no one should be turned away from rallies, etc, because they are not wearing a correct hat – providing the hat they are wearing is serviceable, and that it fits correctly.

- A number of different BSI 4472 hats, in the style of a hunting cap, are already available. **All hats which bear the BSI 4472 mark and the 'kite mark' are acceptable to the Pony Club**. Some do not have a drawstring or the interior padding of a jockey skull and will probably fit only one oval shape of head. Oval shapes of hat differ according to the respective manufacturer, and you should select the one that provides the best fit. *If it has a drawstring it is essential that it is correctly adjusted;* a qualified retailer will help you to ensure that the adjustment is satisfactory.

- Whichever BSI standard 4472 hat you choose, it must have a correctly adjusted harness (chin strap), or it will not fulfil its function.

- Silks or hat covers must be black or dark blue, except for cross-country, when you can wear a silk in the colour of your own choosing. Silks should be fitted to cover the whole skull, with the

A correctly fitted jockey skull with harness and 'silk' cover.

peak horizontal. The tied ends should be tucked away neatly and not left with the bow protruding.

- Never wear a crash hat or hunting cap that is badly worn or damaged.

HAIR

Boys and Girls

- Hair should always be tidy, with no stray strands hanging down over your eyes.

Girls

- Hair must always be worn in a net, well away from your collar; if it hangs over the collar it flops up and down, giving an impression of untidy riding and showing up any defects in the rider's balance and rhythm.
- Longish hair should be put up into a bun. If you insist on wearing a pony tail, it must be tied with a plain, dark band.
- Very long hair should be plaited, secured with a dark elastic band, and – preferably – twisted into a bun.
- On no account should fancy ribbons or brightly coloured slides be worn.

JEWELLERY

This should not be worn at any time. The only exception is a plain bar tie-pin. Earrings, however small, should never be worn when riding, as they are positively dangerous: they can get caught in branches of trees, or in your jacket collar or chinstrap, etc, and can cause very nasty injuries to your ears.

Very long hair should be plaited (above) and worn in a bun with a hairnet (above and below). Far left: how not to look!

JACKETS

RIDING JACKET. A well-made, lined riding jacket protects you against the weather; when you are riding through woods, etc; and also in a fall. It should be made of a serviceable brownish or greeny-grey tweed (sometimes called Derby or Keeper's tweed) or covert cloth in a style specially designed for riding. It must fit well, never restricting the rider's movements. It should have one or two vents at the back, and should be free from adornments such as velvet collar, fancy buttons or brightly coloured lining.

Tweed jackets are correct wear for all Pony Club activities, including hunting.

HUNTING COAT. See sections on horse trials, hunting and show jumping.

ANORAKS are excellent for riding at home but should not be worn for rallies as it is difficult for an instructor if you wear a bulky and shapeless garment. Anoraks are certainly not suitable for competitions or hunting.

WHAT TO WEAR WITH A RIDING JACKET
- White or plain-coloured shirt.
- Tie (e.g. Pony Club), which should be neatly tied and secured with a plain bar tie-pin.
- Pony Club badge (sparkling clean at all times). This should be worn on the lapel of the riding coat – preferably with no other badges.
- At rallies your DC or Instructor may allow you to wear a dark coloured sweater over a shirt and tie. The sweater should fit well, to show your correct outline when mounted. Many Pony Club branches now have sweaters showing the Pony Club badge and name of the branch. These are practical as well as smart.

SHIRTS

With an ordinary tie a plain shirt with a well-fitting collar is correct. With a hunting tie a shirt without a collar but with a well-fitting neck-band is most suitable.

JODHPURS AND BREECHES

These are designed specially for riding and are close-fitting in the areas which have contact with the saddle and the horse's sides.

They are reinforced in knee and thigh areas for protection and durability. Loose trousers or jeans are unsatisfactory, as they crease or ride up the legs, causing rubbing, soreness and discomfort.

Nowadays stretch materials are generally used; one-way stretch is more becoming than two-way. Fawn is the correct colour for competitions, for showing, and for hunting. Dark colours or corduroy are practical for casual and informal riding; at Pony Club working rallies they may be worn at the discretion of the DC or Instructor. They should never be worn in competitions. Jodhpurs can be worn with an elastic under the foot to keep them tight.

Tights can be worn underneath breeches or jodhpurs for comfort and warmth, and to prevent chafing if you are in the saddle for long periods.

FOOTWEAR

With all footwear for riding it is important for the soles to be smooth and for the heels to be a sensible depth.

- Never ride in 'wellies', 'trainers', or shoes with very ridged soles, as they are likely either to slip through the stirrup or to get caught up should you fall off.

JODHPUR BOOTS (preferably with elasticated sides) are ideal for wearing with jodhpurs, but strong lace-up walking shoes with plain soles and sensible heels are acceptable.

RIDING BOOTS should be close-fitting to the leg, for comfort, neatness and to keep water out.

- They should cover the length of your calf but should not impede your knee joint when fully bent.
- The best ones are made of leather, but rubber ones are a suitable alternative for Pony Club wear.
- Do not necessarily buy the first pair that you try on. Be sure that the fit is satisfactory. Especially with rubber boots, it is a good idea to make allowances for winter wear: i.e. the foot should be big enough to put in an inner sole; this adds greatly to warmth. The leg should fit as closely as possible.
- All boots should be kept clean and polished.

GARTER STRAPS should be worn buckled towards the front of the knee against the seam of the breeches, with the free end of the strap facing outwards, and trimmed if it is too long.

SPURS should have blunt ends, bending downwards. The straps should be the same colour as the boot. The spur should lie along the seam of the boot above the heel, with the longer part on the outside, the buckle close to the spur, and the loose end trimmed to the right length.

Leather riding boots with correctly fitted spurs and garter straps.

NECKWEAR

TO BE WORN WITH A RIDING JACKET

Pony Club members: Pony Club tie and plain bar tie-pin. After you reach the age of about fifteen it is acceptable for you to wear a hunting tie (stock) with your tweed coat. This should be white or in a dark, spotted material, and should be firmly and neatly tied, as shown in the diagrams on pages 17 and 19.

Neckwear for Pony Club members. Left: Dark, spotted hunting tie with plain bar tie-pin. Right: Pony Club tie with plain shirt.

Above and facing page: Tying a hunting tie (method A). There are two correct methods, both of which are shown in detail on the following pages.

TO BE WORN WITH A HUNTING COAT

White hunting tie with plain bar tie-pin. For how to tie, see diagrams.

GENERAL NOTES ON HUNTING TIES

- If the tie is shaped, it must be the correct neck size.
- The tie must be firmly, correctly, and neatly tied. Two correct methods are shown in the diagrams.
- Hunting ties are not suitable for very young riders, as their necks are not long enough and the ties do not fit.
- They have been known to save lives, giving protection in bad falls, and even preventing a broken neck. They can also be used as a tourniquet to stop bleeding if your horse cuts a leg badly.

All neckwear should be washed and ironed after every outing.

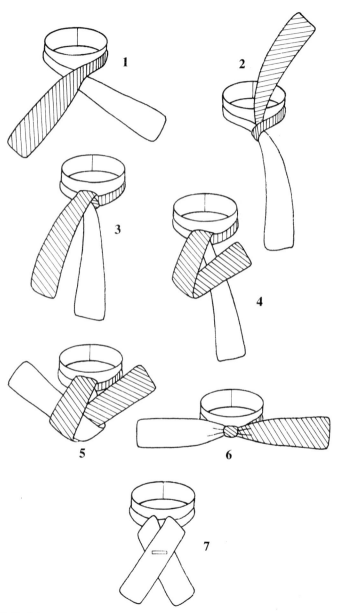

Method A.

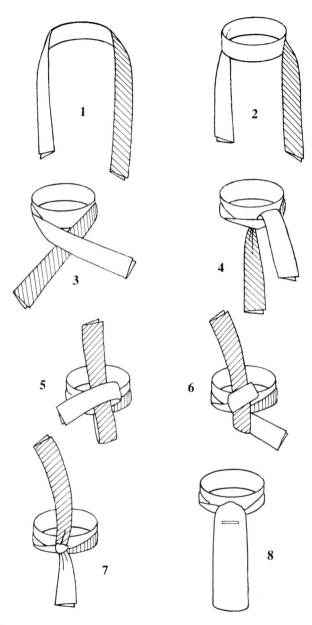

1

2

3

4

5

6

7

8

Method B.

GLOVES

Gloves must be worn for competitions, for shows, and for hunting. They are also practical for protection against the cold and rain, and they provide a better grip when the reins are sweaty; note that for these reasons many top riders wear gloves when schooling.

For dressage schooling, leather gloves are preferable as they ensure a much truer 'feel', though it should be noted that if they get wet the reins tend to slip through them. For other purposes gloves can be made of cotton, string or nylon, either lined or unlined. For mounted work, string gloves are probably the most suitable, as they wash and wear well. Choose gloves which are specially designed for riding.

- Always wear gloves (preferably leather) when lungeing a horse.
- On wet days, carry a spare pair tucked beneath the girth under the saddle flap.

WHIPS

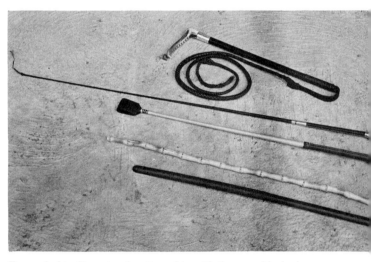

Types of whip. From top, hunting whip with thong and lash; dressage whip; cutting whip; plain and leather covered canes.

CORRECT DRESS FOR YOUNG RIDERS

PONY CLUB ACTIVITIES
WORKING RALLIES

Members and Associates

BSI 4472 crash hat with dark blue or black cover.
Riding jacket.
Shirt with collar and tie.
Sweater or v-necked pullover, without jacket if weather permits.
Jodhpurs or breeches.
Jodhpur boots or riding boots.

Note: This is also the correct dress for Associates when instructing. Associates and Instructors should at all times be correctly dressed, setting a good example to the children they are teaching.

COMPETITIONS

- Before taking part in any competition it is essential to refer to the current rule book.
- Earrings are not allowed in any Pony Club competition.

For Dressage, Hunting, Horse Trials, Hunter Trials, Polo, Show Jumping, Showing, Side-Saddle, see under relevant sections.

PRINCE PHILIP GAMES
BSI 4472 crash hat with dark blue or black cover.
White shirt. You will probably be allocated a tabard in your team colours.
Pony Club tie with plain bar tie-pin.
Jodhpurs (fawn or cream).
Jodhpur boots.
Note: Always check your Rule Book.

TETRATHLON (RIDING)
As for Horse Trials cross-country phase.

Above: Riders wear tabards in their team colours for mounted games.
Left: A hunt sweatshirt may be worn at Pony Club working rallies.

DRESSAGE
Pony Club Members

BSI 4472 crash hat with dark blue or black cover.

White shirt with collar, and Pony Club tie with plain bar tie-pin (tweed coat)

OR

Collarless shirt and white hunting tie with plain bar tie-pin (dark coat), or dark spotted hunting tie (tweed coat).

Tweed or dark blue or black coat.

Jodhpurs (fawn) with jodhpur boots.

OR

Breeches (fawn) with black riding boots.

Gloves (preferably leather).

Whip
Spurs } See Dressage Rules.

Note: Always check the Rule Book, and remember that in all dressage competitions your appearance is very important. Also check that you have the correct tack according to the Rules, which are subject to change.

Older Members and Associates may wear the following:

BSI 4472 crash hat with dark blue or black cover.

Dark blue or black hunting coat.

Collarless shirt.

White hunting tie with plain bar tie-pin.

Fawn breeches.

Black riding boots.

Leather gloves.

Whip.
Spurs. } See Dressage Rules.

POLO
When you first begin to learn polo you can wear your ordinary Pony Club riding clothes, but for what to wear later on, see Adult Section.

HORSE TRIALS
Pony Club Members

DRESSAGE PHASE

BSI 4472 crash hat with dark blue or black cover.

Shirt with collar, and Pony Club tie with plain bar tie-pin (tweed coat).

OR

Collarless shirt and white hunting tie with plain bar tie-pin (dark coat), or dark spotted hunting tie (tweed coat).

Tweed or dark blue or black coat.

Jodhpurs (fawn). Jodhpur boots.

OR

Breeches (fawn) with riding boots.

Gloves.

Whip.
Spurs. } If allowed in Rules.

Note: Your appearance is very important in this phase. There is no point in grooming, plaiting and polishing your pony if *you* look sloppy – with lank, floppy hair and untidy clothes. First impressions are of the utmost importance.

CROSS-COUNTRY PHASE

BSI 4472 crash hat with cover in colour of your own choice.

Long-sleeved shirt or sweater.

Jodhpurs (fawn) with jodhpur boots.

OR

Breeches (fawn) with riding boots.

Gloves.

Whip.
Spurs. } See Horse Trials Cross-Country Rules

Recommended: A firmly tied hunting tie.
              A back or body protector under your sweater.

SHOW JUMPING PHASE

As for dressage. Check the Horse Trials Show Jumping Rules for details about whips, tack, etc.

Note: Always check the Rule Book each year to see if any changes have been made.

Above and right: Correct dress for Pony Club members in the horse trials cross-country phase; white and dark, spotted hunting ties are both acceptable. A back protector may also be worn.

HUNTER TRIALS
Pony Club Members
BSI 4472 crash hat with dark blue or black cover.

Tweed riding jacket.

Shirt with collar. Tie with tie-pin OR collarless shirt with white, or dark, spotted hunting tie.

Jodhpurs (fawn) with jodhpur boots OR breeches (fawn) with riding boots and garter straps.

Spurs if required. They must be blunt, and worn correctly. (See page 12)

Note: Cross-country clothes are discouraged at hunter trials, and incorrect dress is sometimes penalised.

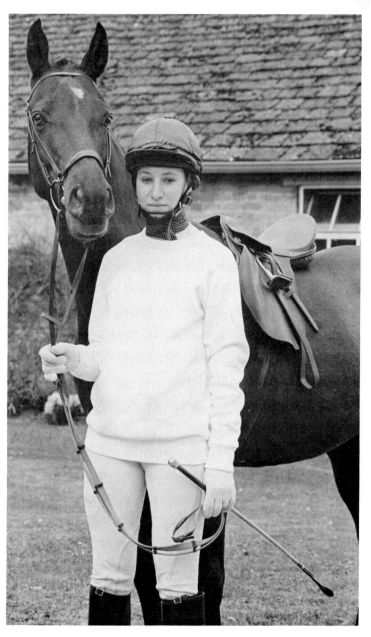

HUNTING

Pony Club Members

BSI 4472 crash hat with dark blue or black cover.

Tweed jacket.

Shirt with collar, and Pony Club tie OR collarless shirt with white or dark, spotted hunting tie (the latter are not suitable for very young members).

Jodhpurs (fawn) with jodhpur boots OR breeches (fawn) with riding boots.

Hunting whip with thong and lash.

Spurs, if necessary.

Note: The above is correct dress until you are twenty-one or have been given a hunt button, in which case you should wear a black or dark blue hunting coat. (See Adult Section.)

Always wear your badge so that the Hunt Secretary can recognise you as a member of the Pony Club.

Below and right: Correct hunting turn-out for Pony Club members.

SHOWING

For showing classes, as in all other aspects of riding or competing, riders should be neatly dressed and correctly turned out. The basics are the same for whichever type of class you are entering:

- Hats should be put on with the brim horizontal to the ground.
- Hair should be neatly tied back or put up in a hairnet. It should never have a 'fringe' showing at the front.
- Boots should be well polished.
- Gloves and a neat showing cane should be carried.
- Too much make-up and jewellery are incorrect and look most unprofessional. So do large buttonholes and bright colours generally.
- Your overall aim must be to complement the horse rather than detract from it, as it is the animal and not the rider who is being judged.

The following is a guide to the accepted correct dress for most of the different types of show class.

CHILDREN'S SHOW PONIES

Dark blue or black hunting cap or bowler.
Dark blue or black hunting coat.
Shirt with collar, and tie with plain bar tie-pin.
Fawn jodhpurs.
Brown or black jodhpur boots.
Dark leather gloves.
Plain or leather-covered show cane.

CHILDREN'S PONIES OF SHOW HUNTER TYPE
WORKING HUNTER PONIES

Dark blue or black hunting cap or bowler.
Tweed coat. (Dark blue or black coats may be worn for final judging at major shows.)
Shirt with collar, and tie with plain bar tie-pin. (Not white tie.)
Fawn (not white) jodhpurs. For older children fawn (not white) breeches.
Brown or black jodhpur boots. For older children, plain riding boots with garter straps.
Whip or cane not exceeding 1 metre in length.
No spurs.

SIDE-SADDLE

Hunting cap. No veil.

Hair ribbons should be black, brown or navy blue only, and should be kept to a minimum.

Side-saddle habit with black riding boots.

Shirt with collar, and tie with plain bar tie-pin.

Leather gloves.

Cane or whip not more than 1 metre in length.

No spur.

Correct dress for a child riding side-saddle.

CARE OF RIDING CLOTHES

Riding clothes are expensive, and in fairness to your parents who have provided them for you, you should care for them properly. The following are some notes to help you.

FOR STABLE WORK AND TACK CLEANING wear an overall or an old pair of jeans and an old shirt. Don't risk spoiling your good riding clothes. Even during saddling up or unsaddling, nasty stains can be caused, which cannot easily be removed. If, therefore, you are already in your riding clothes, wear something over them to keep them clean.

BOOTS
- If you are going out riding in wet weather it is a good idea to sprinkle some talcum powder in your boots before wearing them; it makes them easier to put on, and especially to take them off if they become soaked through.
- Always use trees to keep boots in good shape. When you have eased the tree into the boot, turn the boot upside down and push it over the tree, to prevent wrinkling and to make polishing easier. An alternative to using trees is to stuff the boots with newspaper.

To clean
Wash, wipe with a dry cloth and leave to dry – but not near strong heat, which can ruin the leather. Use a good-quality boot polish. Rubber boots should also be polished after washing; a liquid polish is the most suitable.

Never leave your boots lying about on the floor. Stand them on their own two feet.

BREECHES AND JODHPURS
These should never be left lying around in a dirty condition but should always be washed before they are put away.

HATS
When the hat is not in use, hang it up so that the 'nap' and brim are not damaged. *Never* leave a wet hat resting on its brim for a long

time, as this warps it. Stuff it with crumpled newspaper to keep it raised, or use a wine bottle which makes an excellent hat stand.

To clean

Bowlers, top hats and hunting caps must be dry before they are brushed. Do not brush a top hat or a hunting cap with a brush that is too hard, or you will ruin the velvet or silk.

JACKETS

These should be kept on hangers. Before wearing your jacket make sure that all the buttons are secure.

To clean tweed coats

Use a stiff dandy brush to remove mud, dust, etc. Do not brush coats when they are wet, as mud smears.

To clean dark blue or black hunting coats

Wash down at once with a stiff brush and plenty of water, or brush when dry.

GENERAL NOTE If you are not going to use your riding clothes for some time, brush them and put them away on hangers. In the case of jackets, this may be the time to send them to the cleaners.

DOS AND DON'TS

DO ■ Turn out looking clean and tidy, with your clothes brushed, your boots well polished, and your hair neatly put up.

Wear your hat sitting squarely over your forehead.

Tuck in the points of collars, and pin down your tie.

Trim boot garters or jodhpur boot straps so that the ends do not hang down.

Wear the buckles of your boot garters at the front of your leg and not at the side.

Wear spurs the right way up and on the correct foot.

Wear spurs in the correct place on the boot – not down by the heel.

Wear spur buckles on the outside of the boot not on the instep.

DO NOT ■ Turn out looking dirty and unkempt.

Ever ride without a hard hat.

Wear earrings when riding.

Ride in plimsolls or shoes without heels.

Carry bulky or breakable objects in your pockets while riding.

CORRECT DRESS FOR ADULT RIDERS

DRESSAGE

For all competitions except at advanced and international level the following is correct for men and women:

Top hat.
Dark blue or black hunting coat.
Collarless shirt.
White hunting tie with plain bar tie-pin.
White breeches.
Black boots.
Leather gloves.
Spurs. } See Dressage Rules.
Whip.

For advanced competitions a tail coat may be worn. For international competitions a tail coat *must* be worn.

Women

DRESSAGE PHASE

Novice

Bowler hat or hunting cap.
Tweed or dark blue or black hunting coat.
Shirt with collar, and plain tie with plain bar tie-pin (tweed coat).

OR

Collarless shirt with white
    hunting tie (dark coat) or
    dark spotted hunting tie (tweed
    coat).
Fawn breeches.
Black or brown boots.
Gloves.
Spurs, as in Rule Book.

Intermediate and above

Hunting cap or bowler hat.
Dark blue or black hunting coat.
Collarless shirt.
White hunting tie.
Fawn breeches.
Black boots.
Spurs.
Gloves, as in Rule Book.

OR

Top hat.
Black swallowtail coat.
Collarless shirt.
White hunting tie.
Waistcoat, beige, yellow or
    Tattersall check.
Fawn breeches.
Black boots.
Gloves.
Spurs, as in Rule Book.

Correct dress for international level dressage (left) and for horse trials dressage at intermediate level and over (above).

CROSS-COUNTRY PHASE

Crash hat with cover in colour of your own choice. (Under BHS rules a BSI 4472 hat is compulsory.)

Hunting tie (white).

Fawn breeches.

Long-sleeved sweater or shirt in colour of your own choice.

Black boots.

Gloves.

Whip.
Spurs. } As in Rule Book.

A back or body protector is recommended for safety purposes.

SHOW JUMPING PHASE

Hunting cap with harness or crash hat with dark blue or black cover. (Under BHS rules a BSI 4472 or BSI 6473 hat is compulsory.)

Tweed or dark blue or black hunting coat.

Collarless shirt with white hunting tie (dark coat) or shirt with collar, plain tie and tie-pin or dark spotted hunting tie (tweed coat).

Fawn breeches.

Black boots.

Gloves.

Whip
Spurs } As in Rule Book.

GENERAL NOTES

- You should take great care over your general appearance.
- A top hat or bowler should always be worn with a bun for the most elegant effect.
- Hair should be worn as neatly as possible. Long, floppy hair emphasises any tendency to 'nod' during a dressage test.
- When riding across country, hair should be well tucked out of the way for safety reasons.
- Your hunting tie should be worn correctly, so that the overall effect is neat and elegant. See diagrams on pages 17 and 19.
- The wearing of earrings is incorrect as well as dangerous. In fact no jewellery should be worn, except for a plain bar tie-pin.

DRESSAGE PHASE

Novice

Bowler hat or hunting cap.

Tweed or black hunting coat.

Shirt with collar, and dark tie with plain bar tie-pin (tweed coat).

OR

Collarless shirt and white hunting tie (black coat) or dark, spotted hunting tie (tweed coat).

Fawn breeches.

Black or brown boots. (Brown boots are not worn with a black coat.)

Gloves.

Spurs, as in Rule Book.

Intermediate and above

Top hat.

Black hunting coat.

Collarless shirt.

White hunting tie with plain bar tie-pin.

White breeches.

Black boots with mahogany tops. (Boots without tops are not worn with white breeches.)

Gloves.

Spurs, as in Rule Book.

OR

Hunting cap.

Black hunting coat.

Collarless shirt.

White hunting tie with plain bar tie-pin.

Fawn breeches.

Black 'butcher' boots. (Boots with tops are not worn with fawn breeches.)

Gloves.

Spurs, as in Rule Book.

OR

Top hat.

Red or black swallowtail coat.

Collarless shirt.

White hunting tie with plain bar tie-pin.

A top hat and tail coat may be worn for horse trials dressage at intermediate level and above.

Adult dress for the horse trials cross-country phase. Fawn breeches with black boots may also be worn.

Waistcoat, beige or Tattersall check.

White breeches.

Black boots with mahogany tops. (Boots without tops are not worn with white breeches.)

Gloves.

Spurs, as in Rule Book.

CROSS-COUNTRY PHASE

Crash hat with cover in colour of your own choice. (Under BHS rules a BSI 4472 hat is compulsory.)

Long-sleeved sweater or shirt in colour of your own choice.

White hunting tie.

Fawn breeches with black boots, or white breeches with topped boots.

Gloves.

Whip
Spurs } As in Rule Book.

For safety purposes a back or body protector is recommended.

Right: A back protector.

SHOW JUMPING PHASE

Novice

Crash hat with dark blue or black cover, or hunting cap with harness. (Under BHS rules a BSI 4472 or BSI 6473 hat is compulsory.)

Tweed or black hunting coat.

Shirt with collar, and tie with plain bar tie-pin (tweed coat).

OR

Collarless shirt and white hunting tie (black coat) or dark spotted hunting tie (tweed coat).

Fawn breeches.

Black or brown boots. (Brown boots are not worn with a black coat.)

Gloves.

Whip
Spurs } As in Rule Book.

Intermediate and above

Hunting cap with harness, or crash hat with dark blue or black cover. (Under BHS rules a BSI 4472 or BSI 6473 hat is compulsory.)

Black hunting coat.

Collarless shirt.

White hunting tie with plain bar tie-pin.

Fawn breeches.

Black 'butcher' boots.

Gloves.

Spurs, as in Rule Book.

OR

Hunting cap with harness, or crash hat with dark blue or black cover. (Under BHS rules a BSI 4472 or BSI 6473 hat is compulsory.)

Red or black hunting coat.

Collarless shirt.

White hunting tie with plain bar tie-pin.

White breeches.

Black boots with mahogany tops.

Gloves.

Spurs, as in Rule Book.

Correct dress for an adult in the horse trials show jumping phase. Fawn breeches and black 'butcher' boots may also be worn.

POLO

These notes apply to players of all ages and of both sexes.

For Practice Chukkas

Polo helmet with a secure chinstrap. Pony Club members may wear
a BSI 4472 hat.

Jeans, with or without leather chaps. These are usually acceptable
at most clubs; otherwise, wear breeches and boots.

It is essential to have a white shirt, and a second shirt in the correct
colour of the club for which you are playing: red at most clubs,
blue at Cirencester. At Cowdray Park, yellow vests are provided.

Boots can be black or brown. Buckles must not be worn.

Knee guards.

For Matches and Tournaments

Polo helmet with a secure chinstrap. Pony Club members may wear
a BSI 4472 hat (a BSI 4472 hat is acceptable in all Pony Club
tournaments except the Jack Gannon Trophy).

White breeches. (The wearing of Long Johns or tights underneath is
recommended, to prevent chafing.)

Brown boots, without buckles.

Knee guards.

Team shirt, preferably showing the number of the position in which
you are playing.

Gloves. String or other non-slip glove for the left hand and, if you
wish, a golf or cut-away driving glove for the other hand.

Whip. Correct polo whip: length 36 inches.

Spurs, if necessary. Rowels should be plain, not sharp.

SHOW JUMPING

Broadly speaking, show jumping attire is based on correct hunting
dress. However, certain variations are permissible and readers are
recommended to consult the British Show Jumping Association
Rule Book for the latest guidelines.

SHOWING

HACKS AND RIDING HORSES

Men and Women

Dark blue or black hunting cap or bowler hat.
Dark blue or black coat. Tweed coats are sometimes worn in riding
  horse classes.
Shirt with collar, and tie with plain bar tie-pin.
Fawn or cream breeches.
Plain boots with garter straps.
Leather gloves.
Plain or leather-covered show cane.
Spurs.

COBS, WORKING HUNTERS AND HUNTERS

Men

Bowler hat.
Tweed coat.
Shirt with collar, and tie with plain bar tie-pin.
Fawn breeches.
Plain boots with garter straps.
Leather or string gloves.
Plain or leather-covered show cane.
Spurs.

For major shows, Royal International Horse Show and
  Horse of the Year Show:
Daytime: dress as above.
Evening: correct hunting dress, with hunting whip.

*Left: In show classes for cobs
and hunters, men wear a
bowler hat and tweed jacket.*

*Right: Women may wear a
bowler or a hunting cap when
showing hunters or cobs.*

Bowler hat or hunting cap.
Tweed coat. A dark blue or black coat may be worn for finals.
Shirt with collar, and tie with plain bar tie-pin.
Fawn breeches.
Plain boots with garter straps.
Leather or string gloves.
Plain or leather-covered show cane.
Spurs.

For major shows, Royal International Horse Show and
Horse of the Year Show:
Daytime: dress as above.
Evening: correct hunting dress, with hunting whip.

SIDE-SADDLE

Bowler hat with veil.
Hair in a bun (false if necessary).
Side-saddle habit with black boots.
Shirt with collar, and tie with plain
   bar tie-pin.
Leather gloves.
Cane or whip not more than
   1 metre in length.
Spur.

For finals:
Top hat with veil.
White hunting tie.

Right: A bowler hat worn with a veil.

Left and above: A top hat, with veil, is worn for side-saddle finals. It is also correct to wear a spur.

HUNTING

CUB-HUNTING

This usually begins as soon as the corn is cut (August/September).
Early in the season, cub-hunting is fairly relaxed and the following
  is the accepted dress:
Bowler hat or hunting cap.
Tweed coat.
Shirt with collar and plain tie.
Fawn breeches.
Black (or brown) boots with garter straps.
Hunting whip with thong and lash.
Spurs.

Correct dress for a woman when cub-hunting.

As the cub-hunting season progresses and the opening meet draws nearer, smarter clothes are worn. Although a plain tie is suitable at all times it can now be replaced by a white or coloured hunting tie; dark colours – such as dark blue with small white spots – always look more elegant. The two correct ways of tying a hunting tie are shown in the diagrams on pages 17 and 19. Neatness of turnout is the main essential. It is traditional to wear gloves and to carry a hunting whip with thong and lash.

Accepted dress for a man when cub-hunting.

Men and women may wear a bowler hat for cub-hunting.

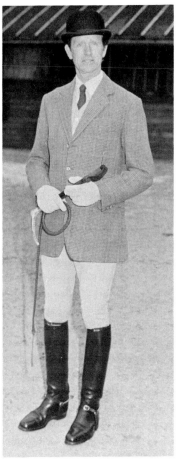

Bowler hat or hunting cap.
Dark blue or black hunting coat.
Collarless shirt.
White hunting tie with plain bar tie-pin.
Waistcoat or dark V-necked sweater.
Fawn breeches.
Black boots with garter straps.
Gloves.
Hunting whip.
Spurs.

Note: Hunting coats should be in a warm material and should have no extra buttons or adornments, but can have one, or two, vents at the back. The lining should always be fawn or dark – not brightly coloured.

Correct hunting dress for a woman.

Top hat.

Red or black swallowtail coat.

Collarless shirt.

White hunting tie with plain bar tie-pin.

Waistcoat, beige or Tattersall check.

White breeches.

Black boots with mahogany tops and white garter straps. (Boots without tops are not worn with white breeches.)

Gloves.

Hunting whip.

Spurs.

OR

Top hat.

Red or black hunting coat.

Collarless shirt.

White hunting tie with plain bar tie-pin.

White breeches.

Waistcoat (optional), beige or Tattersall check.

Black boots with mahogany tops and white garter straps.

Gloves.

Hunting whip.

Spurs.

OR

Hunting cap.

Black hunting coat.

Collarless shirt.

White hunting tie with plain bar tie-pin.

Waistcoat (optional), beige or Tattersall check.

Fawn breeches.

Black 'butcher' boots and black garter straps. (Top boots are not worn with fawn breeches.)

Gloves.

Hunting whip.

Spurs.

Note: The hunting coat should be made of good, thick material, correctly cut, and should have two buttons at the back of the 'skirt', with a long vent and a seam at the waist.

For hunting, a man may wear a cut-away coat (above) or an ordinary hunting coat (right). A hunting coat should have a long vent, two buttons and a seam at the waist (right, inset).

A black hunting coat, worn with fawn breeches and a hunting cap.

Above: A riding hat should always be worn square on the head.

Below: Hat worn on back of head.   *Below: Hat worn at correct angle.*

- If you live in hunting country and have subscribed to the hunt over a certain period you may be given the hunt button by your Master of Foxhounds – in which case you are entitled to wear it. (Sometimes this also entails a distinctive collar.) Until then your coat should have plain black buttons.

- Hats – whichever style they are – should always be worn square on the head, slightly over the forehead, in keeping with their design. They are not to be worn on the back or side of the head, as this impairs their safety factor.

  It is most important to buy a hat that sits firmly on your head so that it won't fall off. If for safety reasons you decide to wear a crash hat, it should have a dark blue or black cover. It must be correctly adjusted for comfort – so do not buy the first one that you try on, but shop around until you find the one that is most comfortable. It can be made to fit snugly by adjusting the lacing at the back.

  Farmers have always traditionally had the right to wear a hunting cap – as do the Master and hunt servants – but because of the safety factor it is becoming more common practice among other members of the hunt. If you do wear one, you must tuck up or cut off the ribbons at the back, as it is the prerogative of the hunt servants to wear them hanging down.

If you wear a hunting cap, cut off the ribbons at the back or tuck them up.

INDEX